THE COVID RECOVERY

Inspirations and Affirmations to Positively Move Forward

Danielle K. Zonca

ISBN 978-1-0980-9672-4 (paperback)
ISBN 978-1-0980-9673-1 (digital)

Christian Faith Publishing, Inc.
832 Park Avenue
Meadville, PA 16335
www.christianfaithpublishing.com

Photography Credits: Dolores A. Stewart, Tammy Day Bishop, Veronica Derme

Printed in the United States of America

Introduction

COVID has affected every single person in one way or another. Many lost loved ones to the deadly infection, while others lost jobs, homes, friends, and a sense of security in their own homes. In whatever way COVID affected you, please realize that you are capable of overcoming the trauma. You can accept it, grieve, and choose to move forward for yourself and your loved ones and still achieve the happy, prosperous life you were meant to live. Faith is a strong word and must be believed when it's applied. Sometimes, one needs to have faith within themselves to understand that they have the strength within them to overcome pitfalls in life. No one is guaranteed their time here on earth. However, we are guaranteed how we choose to live our lives while here on this beautiful, amazing earth.

Sometimes, things like COVID create the ultimate roadblock that can deter us from achieving our goals and purpose. This book was written to assist people to remember their value, the things in which they're capable of achieving, and that we control how we maneuver the hurdles that pop up in our lives. You are never alone in feeling despair or stuck or blocked in some way. At some point in time, everyone feels these emotions during life. The difference is how people choose to understand, accept, and handle them to move forward with an individual path for themselves and their lives. These inspirations and affirmations were created to help you navigate your individual journey and maintain positive thinking to help produce positive outcomes. No two people are the same, so please utilize these positive messages for your own purpose and how they translate to you. "I am fearfully and wonderfully made" (Psalm 139:14 NIV).

1. Is what I'm doing today getting me closer to where I want to be tomorrow?

   I wrote this quote in my private journal in 1997 as a young teenager and lived by it ever since to only learn as an adult that it is very similar to a quote by Paulo Coelho, which states, "Always ask yourself if what you're doing today is getting you closer to where you want to be tomorrow." Wow. Very powerful. If your answer to the above is no, then try taking some time to reflect on what is important to you and where you want to be in the future. Start with defining your goal and then taking the necessary steps and making the appropriate choices to obtain it.

2. If today was the last day I had on earth, would I be proud of who I was today?

   If your answer to the above is no, try adjusting something in your life such as adding a daily good deed or something to benefit others, each day of your life. Add something or remove something that will help you change your answer to yes. Remember, you are capable of answering yes and feeling good about it!

3. It's okay if I don't succeed with all my goals today, as long as I tried and I'm willing and committed to try again and strive for my success.

    At times, we can put too much pressure on ourselves. Remind yourself that you have a goal and that accomplishing the goal doesn't happen overnight. Stay committed.

4. Sometimes we need to write crooked, or in the center of the page, because life isn't always straight pages and even lines.

    Understand that life isn't always perfect, and be ready and capable of adjusting to the pages presented before you. Be open to tackling something in a different way, if/when needed.

5. Make your life a window to allow love to shine through it and then a mirror to reflect that love to everyone you meet.

    Set an example for others *through yourself,* and spread a positive, loving outlook on life.

6. Life is too serious to be taken seriously at all times.

    Allow yourself the fun, nonserious moments when they present themselves so as not to miss out on the joys of life.

7. Have the courage to face yourself every day in the mirror and say, "Thank you," to yourself. Then reflect on all the reasons you have to be thankful for you!

    Many times, we forget ourselves and all the wonderful things we have accomplished and done for ourselves and others. Allow yourself to be grateful for those things, and credit yourself for achieving them. Why is it accepted to thank someone else for something but taboo to thank yourself for doing that same thing *for* someone else? Self-acknowledgment and credit are valuable toward building self-esteem.

8. Remind yourself that you cannot do anything for others if you're not willing and able to first do it for yourself. Do for you first then others because you are number 1 and should first care for number 1.

    This may be difficult to accept. However, think of it in regard to the airline rules if needing to use oxygen masks. You apply your oxygen mask first then assist others because if you can't breathe, you won't be able to help anyone else breathe either.

9. Positive memories are the only gifts worth keeping. Cherish yours forever.

    This applies to precious, happy, and loving memories. Hold fast to them as they are a gift to you since they were made to include you.

10. Have a personal catharsis. Write the words in your mind that no one will ever hear but you. Allow yourself this secret and private purification.

    It's okay to have these private moments for yourself and not share them with anyone. There are some moments that are just meant for you and you only.

11. Stand naked in the noise, and allow yourself to hear everything that's really there. Expose yourself to hear through the noise.

    Vulnerability. Opening up. Blocking out distractions. Be vulnerable if you need to open yourself up, and block out the distractions preventing you from actually understanding what is really there.

12. Through reflection of the past, we can see our future, if we choose to acknowledge it, learn from it, and then apply it.

 If you're not accepting your past and learning from past mistakes, how do you expect to adjust in order to not repeat them?

13. Joy can be felt in the act of forgiving, and it can also be felt in the act of being forgiven! The trick is finding your happy medium to manifest the joy with both so you can give and receive it.

 No one is perfect. Be open to accepting your mistakes, apologizing for them, and learning from them. In return, accept apologies from the mistakes of others. This will help create the balance and joy of forgiving and being forgiven.

14. Hope is a companion throughout your life's journey. It will whisper in your ear to remind you that you're not alone and that the past is over, and you need to open your eyes, not just to see the present, but to behold the future. Open your eyes filled with that hope.

 Hope is defined by a feeling of expectation and desire for a certain thing to happen. Find the hope within you to help you release your past and focus on what may be in your future. Hope is always with you. You just need to allow yourself to feel it and utilize its presence.

15. You are not a bad or selfish person for wanting the best in life. Share that desire, and spread it to others to see where the "ball" rolls next.

 If everyone were to share their goals and dreams with others, it may inspire others to work hard and do the same for themselves without feeling guilty for it. We are all entitled to want the best for ourselves and loved ones. Share it with others to help one another achieve these goals.

16. It's okay to express your emotions. Scream, cry, laugh if you feel the need. Your body is telling you to do it, so allow your body what it needs to release.

    Many times, people will deprive themselves from expressing an emotion. There is a plethora of reasons for doing so; however, if you feel the need to do it, find your private space and let it out. And anyone who tells you that you're wrong or strange for doing it needs to try it themselves one time.

17. Keep a smile on your face behind your COVID mask. People may not be able to see it, but they'll hear it and feel it.

18. And then we cry just a little too loud, and in the silence we hide. Like an empty space in a crowded room, never lost and never found. Where are you?

19. Fill in the blanks for yourself to begin the process of changing negative thoughts into positive ones:

I am _____. I need _____. I want _____. I love _____. My name is _____, and I'm on my personal journey to being the best me I can be.

Example: I am lonely. I need friendship. I want something to do. I love my family.

While on your personal journey to being the best you, how can you change the negative responses to positive ones? Change lonely to content. Change friendship to more time. Change wanting something to do to spend time with others. How can you change your answers to the focus of something positive?

20. "If you always do what you always did, you'll always get what you always got."—Albert Einstein

Take the time to reevaluate things in your life. Do you need to make changes to get where you want to be?

21. Make sure the stars for which you're reaching are actually within reach because otherwise, the fall down is inevitable.

Remind yourself to make realistic goals for yourself. It's great to reach for the stars, but if you don't have a tall enough ladder, your stars will always be outside of your reach.

22. It's okay to walk away if you try, try, and try again and still don't succeed. Not everything is meant to be.

When making reasonable goals for yourself, sometimes, no matter what you try, they just don't come to fruition. Accept it and move on to something else you'd like to try.

23. Give yourself credit and a pat on the back for trying something, even if the results weren't what you expected or wanted. You still deserve credit for trying.

24. Tell yourself, "I love you," today and actually mean it.

    If you can't tell yourself that you love yourself and mean it, how can you say it to someone else and mean it?

25. We get this one life, so make yours count!

    Make it count in your own special ways. Show love to others, teach someone something, spread advice and awareness—whatever counts for you, do it!

26. You are your own greatest asset, and you do not have a price tag!

    Value yourself, and remember that your value is infinite!! While your physical body may have an expiration date, your value and how you use it in the world never expires.

27. How can you expect anyone else to like you if you don't like yourself?

28. Don't ever allow anyone else to make you feel bad about having an emotion. It's okay to get upset about things, and it's your emotion to have, in your moment, and no one else's business or concern.

29. What happens when you shake a bottle of something carbonated? It explodes. If you don't release your feelings and emotions over time, and keep shaking them, you will eventually explode too.

30. No one ever got in trouble for minding their own business. Unless it's a life-or-death situation, or you were asked to be involved specifically, mind your own business.

31. If you act like a jerk, don't question when you're treated like one.

32. Everyone's "key" to happiness is different. The "key" is finding where yours is hidden and then finding which door(s) it opens.

33. Payback sounds like a great idea; however, it can be an even bigger pain than the original issue when you allow it to consume you. Step back and allow karma to do its job instead of you trying to do it.

    Quick note to self: You may want to immediately act on your emotions regarding something significant in your life that involves others who you feel have done you wrong. Instead of reacting to an emotion, take a step back. Allow the course of fate, life, and karma do its role for you. Never cause trouble for yourself with good intentions of helping someone else.

34. We all enter and leave this world in the same way: through birth and death. How we navigate the in-between is what makes us

different. It's not how we look but how we choose to live our lives. How do you *choose* to live yours?

35. You can never trust anyone if you don't even trust yourself. And why would anyone trust you if they know you don't trust yourself?

    Read this a few times to yourself, privately. Would you trust someone whom you believed didn't trust in themselves?

36. Close your eyes and breathe in a quiet space. Remove yourself from the reality to a create a private moment for yourself. Once you've achieved this, then allow yourself to slowly return to the present reality.

37. Only pause things you're able to rewind and view later. You can pause a movie, rewind it, and then view it over and over again, but you can't do that with a conversation.

    If you only had one last opportunity to have a conversation with someone, however brief it may be, would you choose that conversation or the precious movie/TV show you were watching? Pause what you can, while you can, or forever wonder what your loved one would've said to you prior to passing and leaving this life.

38. Lending someone an ear, listening, and giving advice costs nothing but your time.

    Take the time for a request to listen to someone and give your advice. It's a compliment because it means that person asking values what you have to say and offer.

39. You can never truly forgive anyone if you can't forgive yourself for something first.

40. When you tell someone to have a great day, actually mean it, or don't say it at all.

    Too many times, people say things in passing to each other without even paying attention to what they just said. Why waste your breath to utter words to someone else if you don't stand behind and mean what you're saying to them? Think about that the next time you wish a stranger a great day, because if you don't mean it, don't say it.

41. Say what you mean and do what you say!

    If you constantly say things and then never follow through with what you said you'd do, then people will not trust you or ever take you at your word. Therefore, actually mean what you're saying to others, and then always follow through with the things you said.

42. Just because a living being you loved while alive on this earth has passed away, it doesn't mean you no longer love this person and cherish them. Continue speaking about them in the present tense if that's how you still truly feel. They didn't lose relevance in your life just because they passed onto their next life.

43. Acknowledge those who take their time to acknowledge you.

If someone holds a door for you, or gives you a compliment, say, "Thank you," and try to do the same for others.

44. Write your own pages to your own story. Don't allow anyone but you to write your story. You own it. Get to work and live it.

45. Take the time to choose how you'd like to be remembered once you're gone, and then live your life accordingly to create that future memory of you.

46. Scars are just physical reminders of the injuries you've overcome. Consider calling your scars "beauty marks" instead.

47. The physical body may limit us at times, but our minds are limitless.

48. Every accomplishment, no matter how small, is worthy of credit. Allow yourself the feeling of being credited for every single accomplishment you make.

49. A simple acknowledgment of someone's work, attitude, or even struggle can go a long way. Acknowledge someone for something that most people would disregard, and then acknowledge yourself for noticing and acknowledging that person.

50. Everyone appreciates being recognized for something. Be the person to recognize others, and then appreciate the recognition you receive for doing it.

51. Life is full of decisions and making choices. Thankfully, if you make the wrong decision or choice for you, you're afforded the opportunity to make a different one the next time. Nothing but death if final.

    So, you married the wrong person or took the wrong job for you. You still have tomorrow to do what's right for you. Don't dwell on your mistakes. Instead, learn from them, and apply your new knowledge toward your future decisions.

52. Time—we *never* know how much of it we have. Don't just use your time wisely but *enjoy* it as well.

53. If all you do is compare yourself to others, you'll essentially lose who you really are because you'll have been too busy worrying about comparisons and trying to "measure up" instead of embracing yourself for who you are and focusing on that.

   Don't compare yourself to anyone. Use that time to learn who you really are, and then start applying it to the world. Everyone has something to offer. Find what it is that's yours to offer.

54. Change is inevitable for everyone because the world and life are constantly changing daily, which affects everyone. Therefore, the thought that a person can't change is dubious. If the world is constantly changing, then a person has every opportunity to change as well.

   Don't limit yourself, and understand that you hold the power within you to change the things in your life you wish to change. You can teach an old dog new tricks, and you can "improve" something when it's not broken.

55. Nothing is guaranteed or permanent in life. The sooner you understand and accept this, the sooner you'll be able to leave the past behind and move forward.

Marriage, health, happiness, work, friendships—none of these things are guaranteed or permanent. Accept it and keep going.

56. It is *not okay* for you to believe anyone who tells you that your dreams, hopes, and desires are foolish. It's foolish *not* to have those dreams, hopes, and desires for yourself.

57. You cannot fully live with hatred in your heart. It will always deter you, in some way, all the time. Forgive others, forgive yourself, and allow yourself to remove that hatred and ugliness that has been trapped there. Instead, fill that spot with love and joy, and allow yourself to fully live your own special life without anything, or anyone, holding you back.

58. Everyone has their own, unique quality that provides pure bliss and happiness. Find yours, and give yourself some time to enjoy it. Don't ever ignore it!

59. If you held a mirror to yourself every day, what would you want that mirror to reflect to you?

    What could you do differently to change the reflection you see? How could you reasonably make those changes? Does your reflection show your inner soul, or just your outward appearance, and what do you want to see in your reflection daily?

60. It's okay to stop, put everything down, and pause for five minutes when your body and/or mind is telling you to do so. Respect your body and mind because they will always let you know when they need something, so the least you can do is give yourself a five-minute break.

61. You hold the answers to all your personal questions deep, inside you. It's okay to ask yourself these questions and allow yourself the time and opportunity to answer them.

62. "Nonconform" to the "norm." Do your own thing. You're amazing and unique and do not need to conform to society's "norms."

     Allow yourself the freedoms, which you're allowed to utilize, and think freely for yourself. If you believe something with conviction, then don't cave to the popular ideas. Stand true to yourself and your beliefs.

63. Just because a loved one has left their physical body does not mean they've been taken from your heart. Allow your loved one to live within your heart, even they can no longer live walking on the earth.

64. Who told you that you can't achieve your dreams and/or desires? Where is that person now? Never allow anyone to tell you what you can and can't do or want or shouldn't want for yourself. Always go for your dreams while you have the opportunity.

    If you allow someone to dictate your dreams, hopes, desires, you're allowing them to take it all away. Instead, stand true to yourself, and go for the things you want in life. Live your life—not the life someone else wants you to live.

65. If you continue to put your own life on hold for everyone you care about, eventually you'll be living for everyone but you! It's okay to support loved ones with their dreams and goals, but don't make yourself the one sitting on the sidelines while others achieve their dreams/goals. It's okay to have your own cheering squad while you strive for *your gold medal!*

66. Sometimes, our bodies fail us. We become ill, and there's not much we can do to change it. What we can change is how we think about our physical illness. Would you allow someone to physically restrain you, or poison you, and not do anything about it? Most likely, your answer is *no*. It's the same with illness. Allow your *mind* the control to tell your body how it feels. It will be scary—terrifying—but remember it's *your* body and mind, so only *you* get to control how each part feels. Stay positive, love yourself, thank yourself for getting you this far. Tell your body that it's okay it got sick, but you're there to help guide it through the illness and get well.

Many times, when we get sick, we forget that we're still in control of our bodies. It becomes a war between you and the illness. Remind yourself that you're in control of your body because it's your body! The illness may take over, but ultimately, you still control your mind and how you mentally handle what's happening to your body. Hold tight to that because it can help you get through hard times.

67. There is nothing wrong with asking someone for help. Sometimes, all you need is a kind ear to listen to you or a trusted person to tell you the truth and help you find the solution to your problem. Never feel ashamed for talking to someone about something affecting your life. It may save your life.

68. When you've exhausted every idea and option you have for something, humble yourself enough to seek the advice of someone you normally wouldn't ask or want to ask. It'll be that person who gives you the advice you need.

69. Have you ever wanted something so much that you can taste it, see it, feel it, or hear it? If you can envision it in your mind, then what is stopping you from achieving it? Take your time answering the question and then proceed.

70. Start your day with a smile. Wake up, turn off your alarm, put your feet on the floor and smile! Smile for yourself and the day ahead of you. Smile for your loved ones and for those who can't smile today. By starting your day positively, it'll allow for you to have a positive day.

71. If you feel the need to cry, allow yourself to cry. You may not know why you're crying, and if that's the case, accept it and think that maybe you're crying for someone who can't cry right now.

72. Fear is a normal part of life. Everyone has a fear of something, in one way or another. Whether it's a fear of spiders, snakes, heights, drowning, the dark or even monsters—face your fear(s). Do not allow your fears to control you, your emotions, or decisions. When you allow a fear to control actions in your life, you are only holding yourself back from living your best life. Don't fear living your best life.

73. Fill in the blanks for yourself to the following:

> "My name is _____. I am proud of myself for _____.
> I am ashamed of myself for _____
> _____. I choose to forgive myself for that and recognize myself for what I am most proud of accomplishing. Now that I have acknowledged both things, I choose to move forward with the positive and leave the past where it belongs because I have forgiven myself for it, so the present and future are my only focus now."

74. Never decline a brief conversation or moment with a loved one because it may be the last moment you ever share with them.

75. If you don't really mean it, don't say, "I love you," to someone. Insincerity is noticed by the recipient of your words. Don't say things unless you actually mean them.

76. The saying "Sticks and stones may break my bones, but names will never hurt me" is powerful and true to an extent. However, words can cut and stab a person's emotions/feelings. Be cautious with what you say so as not to harm someone with your words.

77. Perfection does not exist. Dedication, hard work, and determination exist, but even combined, they don't equal perfection. Accept yourself for your imperfections, and credit yourself for those imperfections while relishing in the fact that you always give everything your best. There is no harm in being perfectly flawed.

78. You may not know your true purpose in life yet, and that is perfectly okay. But what is your passion? Can finding your passion lead you to your purpose? Only you hold the answer.

79. Sometimes, people suck and are just plain cruel toward others. You can't control that. What you can control is how you respond to those people. Will you allow their bad attitude to ruin your day, or will you take control and treat them with a positive response and focus on a great day for you instead?

   The choice is yours. Remember, you always have a choice with how you respond to negative, nasty people. How will you choose to respond when something happens?

80. Upon completion of this book, please go back to the very first quote and reread it. Are you doing this yet? If not, why? Remember—only you have the power to be the best you and make your life into what you want it to be. Take hold of your

inner power. Accept critiques and advice from others and learn from them, but never allow anyone to tell you what is right for you or that you can or cannot achieve something you desire, because you absolutely can! Remember that it's acceptable to dream and dream big! It's okay to want things for yourself and to strive for those dreams. You get this one life, so make the most of your life!

Remember the Golden Rule: help others when you're able and live your life for you—not anyone else. Remind yourself to have and create reasonable expectations for yourself, and then hold yourself accountable for them.

Above all, love yourself, love others, and be proud to be you and contributing in all the ways you do to this beautiful Earth we call home. You are loved more than you know!!

"Though an army besiege me, my heart will not fear; though war break out against me, even then I will be confident" (Psalm 27:3 NIV).

"The fruit of that righteousness will be peace; its effect will be quietness and confidence forever" (Isaiah 32:17 NIV).

"I came to you in weakness with great fear and trembling. My message and my preaching were not with words, but with a demonstration of the Spirit's power, so that your faith might not rest on human wisdom, but on God's power" (1 Corinthians 2:3–5 NIV).

About the Author

Danielle K. Zonca is a certified life coach, singer, writer, and humanitarian who holds a BA in fine arts and currently resides in Southwest Florida. She is working toward her PhD in psychiatry after gaining much inspiration from her time working with developmentally disabled individuals as a Medicaid waiver support coordinator and consumer-directed care counselor, along with assisting the homeless population within her community. She was born and raised in New Jersey, where she enjoyed growing up with her parents, two brothers, and multiple Doberman pinschers throughout the years.

After struggling with many serious health issues, losing a younger brother unexpectedly, and having to overcome physical constraints from illness by learning to walk again and become capable of caring for herself again as an adult, Danielle realized that sharing the positive affirmations she utilized during her struggles may truly help others. Thus, she decided to dedicate herself to sharing her experiences, teaching and helping as many people as she possibly can. If even one person is touched by her experience and/or words, then she will feel she has accomplished what she set out to do. She has much gratitude and appreciation for her parents, who always supported her and taught her the necessary tools to thrive in an often difficult world. She credits them for teaching her how to truly love and setting an example of how love should be portrayed.

Danielle wishes the finest for everyone and urges others to strive to be the best they can be. She also wants everyone to know that they are loved and to love themselves and others. She is currently working on another book that details her health struggles and how she was able to overcome the many hurdles that almost took her life on multiple occasions. Her intent with sharing her story is to help others understand their internal strength, the power of faith, believing in yourself, and never giving up on yourself.

Dear Mr. President —

I wish you all the best as you lead our amazing country. May you always be blessed and guided and thank you for giving us everything you have to offer.

Keep Smiling Behind Your Covid Mask —

9 781098 096724

- 2021 -